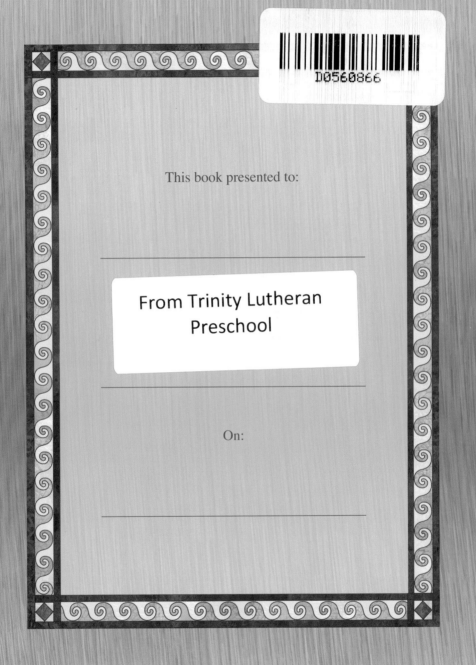

This book presented to:

_____

From Trinity Lutheran
Preschool

_____

On:

_____

Best-Loved
Parables
of Jesus

CONCORDIA PUBLISHING HOUSE • SAINT LOUIS

Arch® Books

Published 2014 by Concordia Publishing House
3558 S. Jefferson Ave., St. Louis, MO 63118-3968
1-800-325-3040 • www.cph.org

Manufactured in Shenzhen, China/55760/411463

Table of Contents

Dear Parents,

Parables are short stories that feature realistic settings, actions, and people. This story form parallels real life and is used to show something about real life.

Jesus used parables to teach His hearers about choices and their consequences and about the kingdom of God and His truth. His parables used situations and people that were familiar to His hearers so they would clearly understand His Gospel message. For unbelievers, though, the meaning of Jesus' parables was locked because these people rejected Him and His forgiveness, mercy, and promise of salvation.

This collection of Arch Books was chosen to teach today's children about six of Jesus' most familiar parables. Each story in this collection will provide you with context so you can help expand your child's understanding of that parable and its significance to his or her own life. Our hope is that this collection serves to expand your child's biblical literacy overall and strengthens his or her faith in Jesus' Gospel message of forgiveness and salvation.

"He who has ears, let him hear" (Matthew 13:9).

The editor

The Wise and Foolish Builders

A Parable of Jesus
Matthew 7:24–27 and Luke 6:47–49 for children

Written by Larry Burgdorf
Illustrated by Paige Billen-Frye

A builder built a house one day
But did it in a foolish way.
He'd found a stretch of level sand
And bought that pretty piece of land.

There was a stream that flowed nearby,
Which sparkled 'neath a sunny sky.
So on that very lovely spot
He built without a second thought.

But then one day the sky went black.
He saw and heard the lightning crack.
Next came some mighty wind and rain.
It almost was a hurricane.

And adding to the general woes,
With all that rain, the stream arose.
It got as deep as it could be
And washed the sand right out to sea.

With no foundation anymore
The house was shaken to its core.
Soon it collapsed and went KERPLUNK!
And turned into a pile of junk!

This is a story Jesus told,
Inviting those whose hearts were cold:
"Repent!" He said. "Believe in Me,
And you will live eternally."

Now there are many people who
Know very well what they should do.
But when it comes to doing it,
They do not do one little bit.

Instead of following what He said,
They turn to other things instead.
"I don't have time for God," they say.
"I'll think of Him some other day."

Some people think that they've been good
And they have done all that they could;
But they are building on the sand
If they think they've kept God's command.

Those who despise the Savior's call
Have no eternal life at all.
Much more than just a house is lost;
Their own poor souls are the true cost.

15

But Jesus talked about a man
Who had a very different plan.
When this man built, he figured out
There would be storms without a doubt.

So he made sure each building block
Was anchored to the solid rock.
Then soon there came the wind and rain,
Which caused the other fellow's pain.

The stream rose up, but come what may,
It could not wash the rock away.
That other house had gone KERPLOCK!
But his was built upon the rock.

In this short story Jesus is
The solid Rock and we are His.
Those who believe in Him alone
Are built upon this Cornerstone.

The storms of life? There will be some.
But on this Rock you'll overcome.
Through all the troubles that you'll face
He'll show you His amazing grace.

When all the storms of life are done,
And life is gone like setting sun,
He'll take you to a splendid place
Where you will see Him face-to-face.

No floods or storms will harm you there;
No sickness, death or worried care.
You'll live forever with the Lord.
The Rock of Ages gave His word.

Dear Parents,

Storms of all kinds can and do occur. These storms take many forms. There are the hurricanes, floods, and tornadoes that wreck homes in just moments. There are wars or terrorist attacks that slowly or suddenly destroy life. And there are the conflicts in our homes and in our own hearts and minds that erode relationships.

Jesus concludes His Sermon on the Mount with the brief parable of the wise and foolish builders. The message couldn't be more clear: "Therefore everyone who hears these words of Mine and puts them into practice is like a wise man who built his house on the rock" (Matthew 7:24 NIV).

When we place our faith and hope in the things of this world and in ourselves, our lives crumble like sand castles. But when we place our faith and hope in Jesus Christ and the solid truth of His Gospel, we can be certain that regardless of the storms that come, the kingdom of God is the one thing that will endure.

The Editor

The Parable of the Talents

Matthew 25:14–30
for children

Written by Nicole E. Dreyer
Illustrated by Susan Morris

Jesus was resting on the Olive Mount
Near the end of His ministry,
When the disciples privately asked their Lord
What the signs of His return would be.

Jesus replied to them, "Keep watch!
You do not know the day."
And then He told them of a man
Who was preparing to go away.

This man was rich, our Savior said,
With wealth and property.
So he gave this order to his men:
"Take care of my talents for me."

The master divided his talents among
Three servants he'd asked to see,
And gave each one a portion of wealth
According to ability.

The first servant called was given five,
The second was given just two,
One for the third. Then their master declared,
"These eight talents I entrust to you."

The master left and Servant One
Said, "I know just what I'll do
I'll put my talents right to work;
To my master I will be true."

Servant Two did exactly the same
And put his two talents to work:
"I'll honor my master's faith and trust;
My duty I will not shirk."

But Servant Three made a foolish choice:
He went home and dug a hole!
"I'll put this deep into the ground
And keep his talent whole."

A long time passed 'til the master returned
And called his servants again
To collect his property and his wealth
And to settle accounts with them.

Servant One showed his master that
He'd turned five talents into ten.
The Second returned not two, but four,
And their master was proud of them.

"Well done, my good and faithful men,
You've done what I expected of you—
Now come and enjoy my happiness
And command many instead of few."

But Servant Three now stood before
The master he knew was hard,
And handed back the talent he had
Only buried outside in his yard.

The master was angry when he saw
What the lazy servant had done.
"Throw him out!" the master roared,
"Give his talent to Servant One!"

Jesus, the Master, has given to us
Abilities He wants us to use.
Each one of us has special gifts;
Which talents belong to you?

Maybe you sing or draw or write
Or could it be that you like to act?
Science and history might be your thing,
Or perhaps you are good at math!

Whatever our gifts that Jesus has given
Here's what He has in store:
When we use our talents to honor Him,
He will bless them and give us more.

Dear Parents,

Ask someone to identify his talents and the response might be something like music or art or sports. When Jesus told His apostles this parable, "talent" was another word for coin. The present-day use of the word talent, meaning having an aptitude for a particular skill, derives from this Bible story. This parable is certainly about the end result of using or not using talent. But when Jesus taught this lesson, He intended it to mean more.

Jesus and His apostles were traveling to Jerusalem for the Passover. In the previous chapter of Matthew, Jesus spoke about the signs of the end of the age, and in the next chapter, the plot to convict and crucify Him is revealed. The Parable of the Talents is preceded by the Parable of the Ten Virgins ("Watch therefore, for you know neither the day or the hour," Matthew 25:13) and is followed by the lesson of the sheep and the goats ("When the Son of Man comes … He will separate people one from another," Matthew 25:31–32). Jesus' earthly departure is clearly imminent and our judgment is inevitable.

In that context, this parable is not about making money or about doing what we're best at. Those things are temporal. It is about what will happen when Jesus returns and how we should spend our time until then. The gifts the Master gives us, in all their forms and according to our abilities, are to be used for His ministry on earth. As God's good and faithful servants, we use our gifts not for our own increase but for the Master's. When we do, our efforts are doubled (and only those gifts from God are increased). Jesus will identify those who have faithfully served Him and will reward them—"Come share your master's happiness"—in the life everlasting. For those who think God is "hard" and who do not use their God-given gifts, their reward will be separation: "into the darkness, where there will be weeping and gnashing of teeth" (Matthew 25:30).

Our Master has given us many talents and opportunities to serve. Talk with your child about his spiritual gifts and about ways he can use them. Model for him your own faithful service in your church and community. As we wait for Jesus' return, rejoice in His presence today in Word and in Sacrament. And "come and share your master's happiness."

The Editor

The Story of the Good Samaritan

Matthew 22:34–40,
Mark 12:28–31,
and Luke 10:25–37
for children

Written by Teresa Olive • Illustrated by Art Kirchoff

An expert in God's law came down
Where Jesus taught one day,
And asked a question of the Lord
To see what He would say.

"'Love your neighbor
as yourself,'
God tells us in His Word;
But just who *is* my neighbor?"
The lawyer asked the Lord.

The lawyer loved his fellow Jews,
But not Samaritans;
He called them "dogs"
   and would refuse
      To even look at them.

Then Jesus told a story
Of a Jew who had to go
On a journey from Jerusalem
To the town of Jericho.

On the way, some thieves jumped out.
They stripped and beat the man
Till he was bruised and bleeding;
Then they grabbed their loot and ran.

The man lay groaning by the road.
A temple priest walked near.
The man groaned louder, but the priest
Pretended not to hear.

Perhaps the priest thought, *What a shame,*
This man is in distress;
But if I stop to ease his pain,
My robe will be a mess.

Next, a Levite came along—
Who helped the temple priest;
But when he saw the wounded man,
His walking speed increased.

The Levite may have told himself
While scurrying away,
"Surely someone else will stop—
I haven't time today!"

The wounded man grew weaker
As the hours dragged on by;
If someone didn't help
  him soon,
It looked like he would die.

Then the poor man heard a sound—
A slow *clip-clop, clip-clop!*
A Samaritan came 'round the bend,
Then made his donkey stop.

The Samaritan did all he could
To help his "enemy";
He bathed and bandaged
    all his wounds,
        And nursed him tenderly.

When the man was strong enough,
The stranger helped him ride
On the donkey, while he walked
Slowly by its side.

It was getting very late,
When—what a welcome sight!—
They saw a little roadside inn
Where they could spend the night.

The next day the Samaritan
Told the owner of the inn,
"I'll pay you well to nurse this man
Till I come back again."

"Now," Jesus asked the lawyer,
"Of the three, which would you say
Truly was a neighbor
To the man robbed on his way?"

The lawyer said, "The one
    who stopped
And helped to ease his pain."
Then Jesus told the lawyer,
"Now go and do the same!"

We all can be good neighbors
Like the Samaritan that day—
Share God's love with everyone
We meet along the way.

Dear Parents:

God commands us to love our neighbors as ourselves. It is only possible to share that kind of love through the redeeming sacrifice of our Savior, Jesus Christ. His love carried Him to the cross in our place. That's the kind of love, strengthened in us by God's Holy Spirit, that flows from Jesus, through us, and to the people around us.

Explain to your child that God calls us to view anyone who needs our help as a neighbor. We don't have to look hard to find a "wounded" person. They surround us in our family, our neighborhood, our church, our country, our world.

With your child, plan a way to share God's love with a hurting person—invite a lonely friend to dinner and a family devotion, donate food and a picture book about Jesus to your church's welfare cupboard, etc. Pray with your child and ask that the people you help will experience God's love as you share it.

The Editor

the Parable of the Lost Sheep

Luke 15:3–7 and Matthew 18:10–14 for children

Written by Claire Miller

Illustrated by Johanna van der Sterre

Here's a story Jesus told
About a sheep, and when it's through,
You will love the special meaning
That His story has for you.

A man who was a shepherd
Had one hundred woolly sheep.
He guarded them the whole day long
And while they were asleep.

He led them where the grass was green,
He found them water too.
He chased the hungry wolves away
And kept his flock in view.

The shepherd knew his hundred sheep,
The lambs, the rams, and ewes.
If they got hurt, he cleaned their wounds,
Each scrape and scratch and bruise.

And when the shepherd talked to them,
The sheep all knew his voice,
So when he called them, they would come—
That was their safest choice.

One day a sheep just wandered off,
And when it turned around,
The shepherd and the sheep were gone!
It didn't hear a sound.

The lost sheep stopped and shook with fright,
It bleated, terrified.
It quickly found a nearby bush
Where it could safely hide.

The shepherd, meanwhile, checked to see
If all his sheep were there.
"Oh, no!" he said, "one's missing now—
I must look everywhere!

"I'll search until I find that sheep
Or it will not survive.
I'll keep on walking, won't give up,
I'll rescue it alive!"

The shepherd hiked uphill and down.
He didn't stop to sleep.
He searched each bush, behind each rock . . .
At last he found his sheep!

The sheep was weak and frightened,
And it couldn't even stand.
The shepherd didn't scold it,
But he calmed it with his hand.

He put it on his shoulders,
And he hurried home so fast,
Then called to friends and neighbors,
"I have found my sheep at last!

"My sheep was lost, but look—it's here!
Let's celebrate—hurray!"
That ended Jesus' story,
But He still had more to say.

Here's the message in His story:
Jesus' love for us is deep,
And He wants us in His family
Like the shepherd wants his sheep.

Like sheep we stray from Jesus
With our selfishness and sins.
But Jesus loves all sinners.
When we're lost, His search begins.

Jesus finds us and forgives us,
And He helps us say we're sorry.
There are shouts of joy in heaven
When the angels hear our story!

Dear Parents,

Most children have experienced the terror of being lost and the relief of being found, so they can appreciate the helplessness of the lost sheep in Jesus' parable. Children may realize that they frequently stray from doing God's will; they sin. When this happens, they are like the lost sheep. But they should also know that naughty children aren't the only ones that stray. The story is about a lost sheep, not a little lamb. All people are sinners, including parents, pastors, and teachers.

The shepherd in Jesus' parable searched for the lost sheep until he found it. He didn't say, "Let it find its own way back"; he didn't give up. And God doesn't give up on sinful people either.

The story demonstrates that God's grace in Christ is unconditional, just as the shepherd's love for his sheep was unconditional. You can use this story to help your child understand that God doesn't reject sinners. He loves them and wants them to remain a part of His family. Just as the sheep in this story did nothing for the shepherd, we can do nothing to earn Jesus' love, and in no way do we deserve to be rescued. Remind your child that Jesus paid a high price to rescue us. His death on the cross for our sake was the ultimate rescue of all lost sheep.

Through the power of the Holy Spirit, we are able to be rescued and repent of our sins. Jesus assures us that just as there was joy among the friends of the shepherd, there is also joy in heaven when sinners repent. Help your child see that our faithfulness to our Good Shepherd is a source of joy to Him.

The Author

The Lost Coin

A Parable of Jesus

Luke 15:8–10 for children

Written by Nicole E. Dreyer

Illustrated by Roberta Collier-Morales

Jesus traveled from town to town
And everywhere He walked,
Crowds would gather and follow Him
To listen as He talked.

The crowds were full of people who
Loved Jesus very much.
They ate with Him and talked with Him
And were blessed by His Words or touch.

But not everyone who followed the Lord
Was happy with what they heard.
They muttered and complained behind His back.
And Jesus heard every word.

The teachers and the Pharisees
Thought Jesus had made a mistake
Because He ate with those who sinned
And collectors with taxes to take.

But Jesus knew these Pharisees
Did not know why He came,
So Jesus told this parable
His gospel to explain:

"Suppose there was a woman who,"
Our Savior began to say,
"Had saved ten silver drachmas—coins—
Each one worth one day's pay.

"But then one day to her surprise
The woman had quite a shock.
One of her coins had disappeared—
Now where could it have dropped?

"The woman's house was very dark—
No windows in any wall.
The floor was earthen—made of dirt—
So the color was rather dull.

"How could she find just one small coin
On a floor made out of dirt?
She lit her lamp, then took her broom,
And swept to begin her search.

"She swept the broom across the floor
And listened for any sound.
Then suddenly she heard the clink
Of her coin there on the ground!

81

"Oh, what joy the woman felt
To have her coin again!
'I'll celebrate,' the woman thought,
'And invite my neighbors and friends!'

" 'Rejoice with me,' the woman said
To everyone she knew.
'The coin I lost has now been found;
I'll share my joy with you!' "

Now you might think it's rather strange
To party for a coin.
But for this woman it was worth
A treasure chest of joy!

Then Jesus told the gathered crowd
Just what His parable meant:
"The angels of God will *always* rejoice
Whenever a sinner repents."

And surely that party up in heaven
Is filled with joyful sounds
Since Jesus came to seek the lost
Wherever we are found!

Yes, *we* were the lost that Jesus found.
He's claimed us as His own
And rejoices over each one of us
Before His Father's throne!

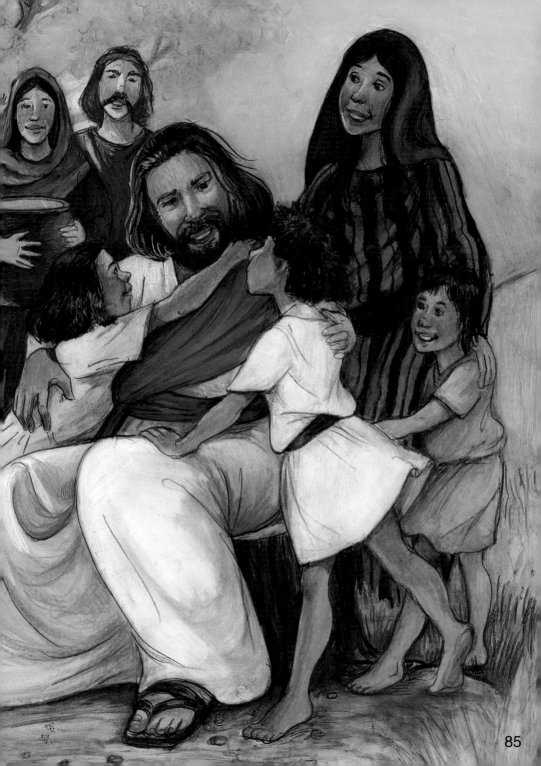

85

Dear Parents,

Although we may not be aware of it, many of us can be quick to point out other people's faults. When we do this, we are just like the Pharisees in this story who were critical of Jesus because He associated with sinners. The Parable of the Lost Coin is a reminder to us that Jesus was sent not to condemn those who do wrong, but to save them. This parable tells us that Jesus came to save all of us, not just the people who think they are good because they do good things on earth; therefore: "... there is joy before the angels of God over one sinner who repents" (Luke 15:10).

A person who repents is one who hears God's Law and recognizes his or her own sin. The person is sorry for what he did wrong and resolves to follow God's Word. Redemption comes by God bestowing His forgiveness upon the penitent sinner. This message of redemption is repeated throughout Scripture. Again: "Just so, I tell you, there will be more joy in heaven over one sinner who repents than over ninety-nine righteous persons who need no repentance" (Luke 15:7).

When you read this story with your child, compare how the woman felt when she found her lost coin to the happiness we feel in recovering something that we missed. Tell your child that every time we do this, we can remember how happy the Lord is when we are "found" by Him and He gives us His forgiveness.

Tell your child that, just as you forgive her when she does wrong things, Jesus forgives us when we ask Him. Explain that because of Jesus' death and resurrection we all, despite our sins, can be saved.

The Editor

Jesus' parable
from Luke 15:11–32
for children

The Parable of the Prodigal Son

Written by Erik Rottmann

Illustrated by Shawna J.C. Tenney

Wherever our Lord Jesus went,
Large crowds would gather near.
The rich and poor and high and low
All pressed around to hear.

The tax collectors loved to come,
And other sinners too.
But Pharisees would shake their heads:
"This simply will not do!

"This fellow welcomes lowly folk!
He even shares their meals!"
So Jesus told a parable
Declaring how God feels:

There was a man who had two sons.
The younger said one day,
"I want my share of your estate,"
Then turned to go away.

The father tried to stop his son.
The boy insisted, "No!"
So father sadly watched his child
Take everything and go.

This younger son spent all his gold.
New friends said, "You're the best!"
But when his money all was gone,
His new friends quickly left.

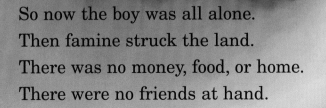

So now the boy was all alone.

Then famine struck the land.

There was no money, food, or home.

There were no friends at hand.

Because the boy fell into need,
He found a lowly job:
A farmer sent him to the fields
To feed his hungry hogs.

The pigs ate pods—much better food
Than this boy had to eat.
His stomach felt so empty that
The pods seemed like a treat.

When he had suffered many days,
The boy said to himself,
"I must return to home again
To live like hired help.

"I am not worthy anymore
To bear my father's name
For I have squandered every gift,
And I accept the blame.

"I hope my father takes me back
To be his hired man.
If he will let me work for him,
I'll never leave again."

But while the boy was still afar,
His father saw him come.
He ran with joy to greet his child:
At last, the boy was home!

The father told his servants, "Go!
Bring him a golden ring!
Let's put the best robe on my boy!
Let's feast and dance and sing!"

Just as this father hugged his child
And brought the boy back in,
So God the Father welcomes you,
Forgiving all your sin.

When God made you His own in Christ,
He gave you His best robe:
He wrapped you in His Son, our Lord;
He cleansed and made you whole.

Dear Parents,

"His father saw him and felt compassion" (Luke 15:20). The Parable of the Prodigal Son (Luke 15:11–32) could also be called the Parable of the Forgiving Parent. A father patiently loves two sons: the younger, who sinfully ran away, and the older (not mentioned in this Arch Book), who sinfully resented both his younger brother and his father. Both sons needed repentance and forgiveness—and their father wholeheartedly forgave both of them! This parable provides you with a clear and simple way of teaching your children about the forgiveness our heavenly Father has for us on account of Christ's death and resurrection. Whenever we fall into sin, our Father in heaven welcomes us back in Christ!

This parable also illustrates how human parents will always love, forgive, and welcome their children, no matter what sins the children might commit. You could use this parable to discuss the suffering the younger son experienced because of his sin. Also focus your child's attention on the forgiveness the father gave, despite the son's rebellion. Such forgiveness does not give children permission to rebel! However, you can use this parable to assure your children that they are always loved and forgiven—by you and by our heavenly Father as well.

The Author

The Arch® Book Bible Story Library

Bible Beginnings

59-1577	The Fall into Sin
59-1534	The First Brothers
59-2206	A Man Named Noah
59-1511	Noah's 2-by-2 Adventure
59-1560	The Story of Creation
59-2239	Where Did the World Come From?

The Old Testament

59-1502	Abraham's Big Test
59-2244	Abraham, Sarah, and Isaac
59-2229	Daniel and the Lions
59-1559	David and Goliath
59-1593	David and His Friend Jonathan
59-2220	Deborah Saves the Day
59-1543	Elijah Helps the Widow
59-2251	Ezekiel and the Dry Bones
59-1567	The Fiery Furnace
59-1570	God Calls Abraham . . . God Calls You!
59-1587	God Provides Victory through Gideon
59-1523	God's Fire for Elijah
59-1542	Good News for Naaman
59-2223	How Enemies Became Friends
59-2247	Isaac Blesses Jacob and Esau
59-1538	Jacob's Dream
59-1539	Jericho's Tumbling Walls
59-2246	Jonah, the Runaway Prophet
59-1514	Jonah and the Very Big Fish
59-2233	Joseph, Jacob's Favorite Son
59-2216	King Josiah and God's Book
59-1583	The Lord Calls Samuel
59-2219	Moses and the Bronze Snake
59-1607	Moses and the Long Walk
59-2266	The Mystery of the Moving Hand
59-1535	A Mother Who Prayed
59-2249	One Boy, One Stone, One God
59-2253	Queen Esther Visits the King
59-2211	Ruth and Naomi
59-1600	Samson
59-1586	The Ten Commandments
59-1608	The Ten Plagues
59-2263	The Tower of Babel
59-1550	Tiny Baby Moses
59-1530	Tried and True Job
59-2260	The 23rd Psalm
59-1603	Zerubbabel Rebuilds the Temple

The New Testament

59-1580	The Coming of the Holy Spirit
59-2259	The Great Commission
59-2207	His Name Is John
59-1532	Jailhouse Rock
59-1520	Jesus and the Family Trip
59-1588	Jesus Calls His Disciples
59-2215	Jesus Shows His Glory
59-1521	Mary and Martha's Dinner Guest
59-2227	Paul's Great Basket Caper
59-2267	The Pentecost Story
59-1578	Philip and the Ethiopian
59-1601	Saul's Conversion
59-1574	Timothy Joins Paul
59-2222	Twelve Ordinary Men
59-1599	Zacchaeus

Arch® Book Companions

59-2232	The Fruit of the Spirit
59-1609	God, I've Gotta Talk to You
59-1575	The Lord's Prayer
59-1562	My Happy Birthday Book

Christmas Arch® Books

59-1579	Baby Jesus Is Born
59-1544	Baby Jesus Visits the Temple
59-1553	Born on Christmas Morn
59-2261	The Christmas Angels
59-1605	The Christmas Message
59-2225	The Christmas Promise
59-1546	Joseph's Christmas Story
59-1499	Mary's Christmas Story
59-1584	My Merry Christmas Arch® Book
59-2252	Oh, Holy Night!
59-1537	On a Silent Night
59-2243	Once Upon a Clear Dark Night
59-2234	The Shepherds Shook in Their Shoes
59-1594	Star of Wonder
56-2209	When Jesus Was Born

Easter Arch® Books

59-1551   Barabbas Goes Free
59-2205   The Centurion at the Cross
59-1516   The Day Jesus Died
59-2213   The Easter Gift
59-2221   The Easter Stranger
59-1602   The Easter Victory
59-2265   From Adam to Easter
59-1582   Good Friday
59-1585   Jesus Enters Jerusalem
59-1561   Jesus Returns to Heaven
59-2248   John's Easter Story
59-1592   Mary Magdalene's Easter Story
59-1564   My Happy Easter Arch® Book
59-2258   The Gardens of Easter
59-2231   The Resurrection
59-1517   The Story of the Empty Tomb
59-1504   Thomas, the Doubting Disciple
59-1501   The Very First Lord's Supper
59-1541   The Week That Led to Easter

Parables and Lessons of Jesus

59-2257   Jesus and the Canaanite Woman
59-1589   Jesus and the Woman at the Well
59-1500   Jesus Blesses the Children
59-1595   Jesus, My Good Shepherd
59-2245   Jesus Teaches Us Not to Worry
59-1540   Jesus Washes Peter's Feet
59-2264   The Lesson of the Tree and its Fruit
59-1606   The Lost Coin
59-2235   The Parable of the Ten Bridesmaids
59-2218   The Parable of the Lost Sheep
59-2224   The Parable of the Prodigal Son
59-2262   The Parable of the Seeds
59-2210   The Parable of the Talents
59-2254   The Parable of the Woman and the Judge
59-2250   The Parable of the Workers in the Vineyard
59-1512   The Seeds That Grew and Grew
59-1503   The Story of Jesus' Baptism and Temptation
59-1596   The Story of the Good Samaritan
59-2214   The Widow's Offering
59-2208   The Wise and Foolish Builders

Miracles Jesus Performed

59-1531   Down through the Roof
59-1568   Get Up, Lazarus!
59-1604   The Great Catch of Fish
59-1581   Jesus Calms the Storm
59-1598   Jesus' First Miracle
59-2230   Jesus Heals Blind Bartimaeus
59-2255   Jesus Heals the Man at the Pool
59-2236   Jesus Heals the Centurion's Servant
59-2226   Jesus Wakes the Little Girl
59-1597   Jesus Walks on the Water
59-1558   A Meal for Many
59-2212   The Thankful Leper
59-1510   What's for Lunch?